A.D. HEWITT

CONFESSIONS

This edition first published in paperback by
Michael Terence Publishing in 2022
www.mtp.agency

Copyright © 2022 A.D. Hewitt

A.D. Hewitt has asserted the right to be identified as
the author of this work in accordance with the
Copyright, Designs and Patents Act 1988

ISBN 9781800943711

No part of this publication may be reproduced, stored
in a retrieval system, or transmitted, in any form or
by any means, electronic, mechanical, photocopying,
recording or otherwise, without the prior
permission of the publisher

Cover image
Copyright © JagCZ
www.123rf.com

Cover design
Copyright © 2022 Michael Terence Publishing

Contents

Synopsis 1

Chapter 1: Confessions 2

Chapter 2: Midnight Love 6

Chapter 3: The Ravers 9

Chapter 4: Nicole's Disappointments 13

Chapter 5: Nicole's Religious Beliefs 16

Chapter 6: Nicole's Confessions 19

Chapter 7: The Barbecue 22

Synopsis

Nicole lived a teenage life of sin!

One day she went to confessions. The confessor confessed to the priest. Subsequently, Nicole became converted! Now her life has changed for the better. Her experience of confessions is a good memory.

Nicole's life will never ever be the same ever again!

Chapter 1:

Confessions

Nicole, a secretary coming from work, came to see her friend Jessica at her house. On a cold winter's day.

Together they both sat in front of the fire in the lounge.

Nicole sat cross-legged, wearing beautiful black stockings and stilettos.

They both warmed up in the heat. They took comfort in the luxury of relaxing both together.

Nicole leaned forward. She reached out to get chocolates from a box of chocolates. From a tray of chocolates, Nicole took a few chocolates. Her favourite ones from the assortment of chocolates. Nicole ate the chocolates. She felt rather aphrodisiac.

"How are you today?" asked Jessica.

"It's not good. I have had a bad day. My life is a mess. I have been ditched. Both my parents are divorced. My mum has no morals. She's having a fling. I don't know what I am going to do. I will go to confessions," groaned Nicole.

"You're wayward," remarked Jessica.

"Do you think so? It must run in the family."

"Why are you going? You're not a bad person."

"I must go. It's a spiritual thing."

"Are you superstitious? What have you done wrong?" asked Jessica.

"I just feel bad. One Sunday I went to church. The pastor said repent of your sin. Ask Jesus into your life."

"Are you ready for this?"

"I don't know. I feel bad. It's awful. I can't explain it," replied Nicole.

"I don't believe it personally," doubted Jessica.

"You like to have fun. You're a hedonist."

"I wouldn't go to that extreme. My ethics are not hedonistic. I do like to have a good time," Nicole's remark was unprovocative.

"You're just like your mother!" retorted Nicole.

"I am not a Christian. I don't think I am that bad. I am not good either. You do have morals."

Nicole opened her compact case. She looked at herself in the mirror. She took a moment to admire her beauty.

"That's one thing I do have," admitted Nicole.

With unashamed Jessica admitted.

"I dabble in the Occult."

"You're a witch."

Nicole felt something brushing her legs. Suddenly the cat curled up by Nicole's feet. The cat moved away. Going somewhere else.

"That shouldn't make any difference to our friendship," said Jessica.

"I hope we are still friends. I see the light. I can't compromise."

"I wish you well with your confessions."

"I am not looking forward to it. It's nerve-racking," said Nicole anxiously.

"It should be okay. You will be alright."

"What will the priest do?"

"He will listen to your confession, of course," answered Jessica.

"That should be interesting. What will he think?"

"You're confessing. Rather you than me," paused Jessica. "Don't worry. It will be okay. Are you sure you want to do this? You don't have to."

Nicole insisted on confessions.

"I do want to go to confessions."

Jessica was apathetic about confessions. She did encourage Nicole to attend confessions.

"Well go!" urged Jessica.

Nicole rose. Holding her folded coat. She put on her raincoat. Her black raincoat was slinky on her figure.

"I must go now. I will see you."

Jessica showed her friend out of the house.

In the driveway, Nicole got in her car. In the pouring rain, Nicole drove off. Going back home.

At the chapel, Nicole attended confessions. In a confession box, the confessor confessed to the priest.

"I lie. I cheat. I am bad. I do wrong. Father, forgive me!" repented Nicole.

"My child! You are forgiven. You have repented. Your sins are forgiven!"

Nicole, with tears of joy, looked at the priest with great love and reverence.

The priest raised his hand and blessed the virgin!

Chapter 2:

Midnight Love

Late at night, Nicole came to see Jessica at her house. She made an apology for not coming to see Jessica yesterday because Nicole had to cover for the personal secretary on annual leave.

Already there at Jessica's house were her friends. They belonged to a witches' coven. Tonight, they would together engage in a séance.

Nicole had no intention of joining them. She condemned such things.

Jessica invited Nicole. Jessica welcomed her. Jessica neglected Nicole. Jessica was too occupied with her friends. Jessica spent all of her time with her friends. They all preferred the company of Jessica rather than her. She blamed herself for the disappointment.

Going into another room, Nicole sat down in the sitting room. There in the room were dolls galore. She took notice of all the prettily dressed dolls. Two of them had ribbons tied in the dolls' hair.

Nicole cooled down in the dim room. She felt unafraid. With spiritual discernment, she had awareness.

From her recent confession, making confession with the priest made her invincible, bold and strong. Nicole's sins were forgiven!

Due to her repentance, she has protection from Christ! The blood of Christ!

Suddenly, Jessica came into the room.

"Aren't you going to join us?"

"No," replied Nicole.

Jessica's friends came into the sitting room. They did insist that Nicole should join them.

Nicole declined to join them and participate in a séance.

"You must pardon me. I won't be joining you."

"Why is that?" they asked.

"I can't. I just can't. It is against my beliefs."

Nicole did not condemn them. She had love for them. She had deep love in her heart. At midnight she felt a deep love. A strong love.

Nicole embraced them, one by one. Nicole felt deep love for all of them. She showed her affection.

"You're a Catholic, aren't you?" said Milly.

"Shouldn't you be Catholics?"

"Not us," they answered.

Teresa, extroverted and emotional, said something else.

"I am moving," interrupted Teresa.

Nicole, feeling sad, came up to Teresa. She embraced her with affection.

"I will miss you when you go," said Nicole sadly.

"I will miss you too!" replied Teresa.

Nicole, deeply sad, did shed a tear. Nicole embraced Jessica last. As the last one, Nicole had the most affection and love for her friend.

Nicole quickly left her friend's house. She did not want to stay any longer there. She deeply missed Teresa.

She abhorred the séance tonight.

Nicole got in her car. She drove home.

Chapter 3:

The Ravers

On Saturday evening, Nicole dressed up. She applied makeup. It accentuated her beautiful features. She looked stunningly lovely.

Nicole came out of her bedroom. She came downstairs. She joined her little brother in the lounge.

Sitting down on the armchair, she waited for her friends to come. Nicole felt nervous while waiting. She fidgeted while waiting for her friends to arrive.

Suddenly, the doorbell chimed.

Her brother answered the front door. Her few friends entered the house and came into the lounge. Nicole rose from the armchair. On their arrival, she greeted Jessica, Michelle and Jacqueline.

"Are you ready?"

"I don't want to go. I have been ditched," sulked Nicole.

"Oh! You must go," insisted Jacqueline.

"Shall I?" murmured Nicole.

"Yes. You must go."

They came out of the house. They got in a car. Jacqueline drove them to a downtown nightclub.

That night, the nightclub was crowded with nightclubbers and ravers. It was Saturday night nightclubbing.

At the nightclub, in the seated area, the young women sat at a table. They drank beverages. The men ogled them. Desiring any of them. Their sex appeal and attractiveness attracted them.

One of the women had her cleavage exposed. The other woman had her long legs revealing from the slits of her black skirt. Her legs showed her beautiful black stockings.

"What's the matter? You look down," wondered Jessica.

Sitting opposite, Nicole looked at Jessica across the table.

"I have been ditched," mumbled Nicole.

"C'mon. It can't be that bad."

Nicole still felt deeply upset.

"Why am I here? What am I doing here? I shouldn't have come," muttered Nicole.

With impatience, Jessica had an urge to dance now.

"Shall we dance?" gestured Jessica.

"Me? Dance! You gotta be kidding," blushed Nicole.

"Come on! Let's dance."

Nicole and Jessica rose while Michelle and Jacqueline remained seated as they reclined at the table.

Both Nicole and Jessica went to the dance floor which was flashing with lights. Nicole and Jessica found somewhere to dance on the dance floor. Everywhere else remained crowded with nightclubbers dancing.

Suddenly, a good-looking man appeared from somewhere. He danced well. Nicole lost her inhibitions. She gained more confidence in herself at having the incentive to dance.

Nicole and Jessica danced next to him. The man dancing preferred Nicole rather than her friend.

Nicole became so excited. She desired him. Nicole perspired from exertion. Her slinky dress was sweat-soaked. Her cheeks flushed. Her perspiration from her body and armpits. Her jet-black hair darkened in the lights. Her hair cascading.

Within moments, the man had gone. Did his wife lead him away? Nicole was disappointed with him as he vanished out of sight. She wanted to pursue him. It was too late. The married man had already gone!

"He's gone!" said Nicole disappointedly.

"He liked you. You did like him. He's dishy. You did have a soft spot."

"Oh! I did. I did!" admitted Nicole. "Now he's gone!"

Nicole lost the urge to dance.

Jessica was filled with libido desiring a romance.

Quickly, they both left the crowded dance floor. They went back to their table where they rejoined their friends. They both sat down. Recovering as they lounged about. They regained their breath.

Nicole and Jessica at present were uninterested in their friends' conversation. One of them a professional secretary and another a receptionist.

Leaving the nightclub together, they made their way to the car.

Jacqueline drove them home. Nicole remained moody and tearful during her journey back home.

The driver, Jacqueline, dropped off the passengers. Nicole was the last passenger to be driven home.

Chapter 4:

Nicole's Disappointments

Nicole took today off work. She could not overcome her setback. She did not get the job. She still felt disappointed at being rejected. She stayed in her bedroom. She remained housebound. She sat for hours on her leather armchair. Relaxing in comfort from her position. In the silence of her bedroom where the light was dull.

She pondered on that handsome man nightclubber she encountered on the dance floor at the nightclub. She wished her dreams would come true!

Late in the evening, Nicole's mother came into her bedroom. Mrs Tweed was concerned about her daughter. Nicole worried, sulked and frowned.

"Come down. How long have you been in your room? What have you done today?" said Mother concernedly.

"Not a lot. I have been thinking. I have been doing some soul-searching," replied Daughter.

Mrs Tweed looked at her tearful daughter sitting still.

"You're not crying. Are you?"

"No, Mum. I am hurt. Can't you see? I won't love again. I will never love again," groaned Nicole.

"A fine lady like you? You're likeable. You shouldn't be hurt. Don't you have lots of friends?"

"Mum, I am hurt. I can't love again!" repeated Nicole.

"Oh! You will. You will. Sweetheart, you shall love. You will love again."

"Me? No! I shan't love. I am deeply hurt."

"You will love again. Do give it time. I don't encourage it. Your father doesn't either."

Nicole thought of her possessive father. Her father had an obsessiveness to be protective of his daughter.

"My father discourages it."

Mrs Tweed moved a tear out of her daughter's big eyes.

"Your father wants the best for you. You must understand that."

"Oh! I do understand. I want to do what's right. I don't want to displease my father in any way," sighed Daughter.

"Your father loves you. He cares for you. He's only doing what's right."

Nicole objected to it to some extent.

"I do have a life. I must live my life!" grumbled Nicole.

"Darling, of course, you do," patted Mother.

"I have to get a new job. I am not getting on with my boss," mentioned Nicole.

"Oh! I am sorry to hear that. We are concerned. We worry about you."

"The sooner I get another job the better."

"You needn't worry. We will support you whatever you do. We want the best for you," grinned Mother.

Nicole worried about her job. Her secretarial duties were done by another professional secretary.

"I will quit. I will have to look for another job. The typist is much better than me."

From being despondent, Nicole left her mother to go upstairs to her bedroom. There Nicole sat back down on her armchair. She did feel humiliated and frustrated. She mused on the advances of her boss, a panderer she had been cautious of, and Personnel which she took heed of them. A disciplinary. Complaining about her coming to work late and her ineffectiveness as a secretary. (This company employed professionals, not unprofessional secretaries.)

Nicole stayed up late tonight. Sitting in the dark in her bedroom with a house light shining from a landing. There the bright light reflected in the dark shadows beyond.

Nicole thought of her work and her bitter disappointments!

Chapter 5:

Nicole's Religious Beliefs

On a Thursday evening, there had been a cloudburst. Inside the cosy house, Nicole, Jessica and her brother sat down together in the lounge. Keeping warm sitting in front of the fire. Brendan sat at a direct angle at the fireplace. They warmed up in the warmth. In the spacious room, there was a suite which furnished the luxurious room. It contrasted with the décor.

Nicole relaxed in front of the fire, stretching out her legs. Jessica sat cross-legged and Brendan sat on the settee. He chewed bubble gum. He kept silent while listening to their conversation. Jessica engaged in apologetics. Her beliefs were different. Jessica did have differences in her viewpoint.

"Why are you so keen on confessions? Do confessions make any difference? It's religion, isn't it? Aren't you religious? I don't believe it. You're a zealot. Muslims are fanatics. Catholicism is a religion," expressed Jessica.

"On the contrary. It's a faith. I believe. That's why I went to confessions. To confess my sins. I repented. My sins are forgiven," said Nicole unashamedly.

"What's the purpose of it?" questioned Jessica.

"Confessions are when one commits sins, then it is time to confess. To repent of your sins. The priest listens to the confessor. Your sins are forgiven. The sinner has repented," answered Nicole.

"That's the Catholic way. I am not sure if I believe it. To me, it's just religion."

"You either believe it or you don't. It's quite simple really. You either go to Heaven or Hell!" said Nicole assuredly.

"Are you condemning me?"

"I am just saying. I am telling you of Judgment."

"What Judgment?"

"The Judgment of the Living God. How one soul is condemned to Hell."

"Does that mean me?"

Nicole spoke about Judgment.

"Yes. If you live a life of sin, a life of hell, then your soul could end up in Hell!"

"How do you know for sure? Quite frankly, you're not much better than me, are you? Don't you sin yourself?" protested Jessica.

Nicole wasn't in the mood to converse with Jessica about apologetics. Nicole kept silent. She did not say anything else therefore to avoid apologetics.

Her confused brother listened to their religious conversation on Theology. Brendan preferred to stay quiet. He did not say anything.

Leaving the house, Jessica had been picked up by her father. On their arrival, they had been punctual.

Feeling tired, Nicole stood by the doorway. Standing still on a doormat, she watched them both go.

Jessica's father drove off home in the van. (During his short journey there, he had earlier dropped off two passengers back to their house in a suburb.)

Chapter 6:

Nicole's Confessions

Out on the patio, Nicole and Jessica sat at the garden table. They sat under the parasol.

During the afternoon, the weather became hotter. The sunshine was radiant. This summer's day was the hottest weather.

They were both refreshed from drinking a glassful of orange juice each. The zesty taste of it was tangy.

Brendan coming home avoided his sister and her friend. He was miserable at having failed his examinations. They both wondered if he failed his mocks. Jessica did not question her brother about his report. Jessica had forgotten about it.

"Now tell me about your confessions," said Jessica.

"What do you want to know?"

"Tell me any of your confessions."

"Well. Let me think. It's a tell-tale. I do have many confessions. Some I prefer not to tell. If I have to tell any. I would reveal this. My following confessions. Once, on my holiday, I sunbathed on the terrace. I got myself a golden tan. I didn't care what anyone thought of me when they saw me sunbathing. I had no inhibitions. I was just like a sunbather sunbathing around the pool getting a tan. Another confession I have is this. Once, I was a desperate secretary looking for promotion and perks that I resorted to stripping in front of my boss. My boss told me to put my clothes back on. I obeyed my boss. Undressing, I was cool and unashamed. Unfortunately, my job did not last long. My boss went to another company. I had to look for another job. At that time, I was a desperate young secretary looking for work and trying to compete," gasped Nicole.

"That's expected. It's nothing new. I know women who try to do modelling. They aspire to be models. None of them will make it."

Suddenly, Jessica's father came home from work.

Nicole kept silent in his presence. She did not blurt out anything else. As soon as Nicole became obtruded on and intruded on and the moment when Brendan imposed on his sister. Then she decided to leave to go home. She disliked talking further in their intrusive presence. She did object to their intrusion. Her privacy was invaded again.

On another June day at Jessica's house, Jessica and Nicole were both alone together in the garden. They both walked together around the garden. Admiring the garden.

"Do you have any confessions?" asked Nicole.

"Not really," replied Jessica.

"Surely you must have."

Jessica confessed to making a confession.

"When I was once a kid, I used to shoplift. I once stole a doll from a toyshop."

"You're naughty. You did have the guts."

"Oh, I did. At that age, I was deprived. My things were hand-you-down." Paused Nicole. "My parents couldn't afford to buy me things."

"I am lucky. My parents provided for me. I was spoilt," admitted Nicole.

They ended their short conversation.

Nicole left to go home. She preferred not to blurt out. She intended to confess to only a few of her confessions. (The confessor did confess to the priest at a confessional box at the chapel.)

Chapter 7:

The Barbecue

Nicole went to Yvonne's house. There she met some of her friends. There in the garden, they had a barbecue on that hot summer's day. The weather was sweltering.

"I hear that you went to confessions," said Gina.

"Oh, I did."

"Did it make any difference?"

"Oh, it did. I am much better now. I have repented. I am a Catholic. I know Catholics who are already practising Catholics. It doesn't seem odd anymore. I could now relate to it. To my situation," answered Nicole.

"We are not Catholics," said Sally.

"I don't believe. I am sure people have their own beliefs," said Tracy.

Nicole's confessional conversation was of a spiritual nature.

"Going to confessions was an experience. It has changed my life. I am a believer! I have confessed. I am forgiven. Now that I have repented. Now I am a Catholic!"

At the get-together, they ate a nice barbecue. Sweating from the heat. Nicole stayed a short time at her friend's house. Feeling nausea and a lack of appetite, Nicole decided to leave to go home.

Her experience of confession was a pleasant one. The confessor redeemed and beatific!

As a recent convert, Nicole had devotion to her Lord. She had faith. She couldn't compromise with all her friends' ways. Nowadays she spent less time with her friends, witches. She knew she would end up losing them, it was inevitable. Her friends thought Nicole was religious. They tried to corrupt her as well as lead her astray. Of course, Nicole felt invincible and formidable being devoted to God. Nicole fretted. She was unafraid of Witchcraft. Her life had changed for the better. Nicole was deeply spiritual and a follower of Christ. With a devotional love for her Lord!

At home, Nicole sat with Jessica in the living room. Nicole preferred to be alone with her friend. Her brother, Brendan, had his friends coming around to his house. Nicole preferred to avoid them. Nicole's conversation was about her confessional.

"I must admit, I am unashamed to be a Catholic. Having gone to confessions."

"Yes, it's a good thing. But don't you see yourself as being holier- than - thou?"

"No. You're all living sinful lives. Personally, I couldn't go on like that. I had to change. I had to make my confessional."

"I respect you. I respect what you have done. You must accept it, that we don't believe. Neither of us," doubted Jessica.

"I am not a good Catholic. I am far from it. But I do believe. I am a believer. It's a shame you can't see the light. You're in darkness. All of you. Your souls in damnation!" condemned Nicole.

"Here you go again! You're no better. Are you?" Protested Jessica.

"All I can do is pray. That your souls will be saved!"

As soon as Brendan's friends come around, Jessica arose and left Nicole's house immediately. Jessica had enough of religious talk and apologetics. Jessica considered Nicole to be a hypocrite. Jessica did not protest at condemning Nicole's hypocrisy, Nicole's hypocritical ways. When Jessica had gone. Nicole remained seated. She prayed. Nicole was deeply prayerful and contemplative. She prayed for her friends. Dark days lay ahead…

- THE END -

*Available worldwide from
Amazon and all good bookstores*

www.mtp.agency

www.facebook.com/mtp.agency

@mtp_agency

www.ingramcontent.com/pod-product-compliance
Lightning Source LLC
LaVergne TN
LVHW021746060526
838200LV00052B/3496